DEPARTMENT OF THE NAVY
HEADQUARTERS UNITED STATES MARINE CORPS
WASHINGTON, DC 20380

I0409645

Standing Operating Procedures for Marine Corps Air Station Search and Rescue (SAR) Units and Helicopter SAR Crewmember Evaluation and Training Program

DEPARTMENT OF THE NAVY
HEADQUARTERS UNITED STATES MARINE CORPS
WASHINGTON, DC 20380

MCO 3130.2
ASA-2A
15 July 1987

MARINE CORPS ORDER 3130.2

From: Commandant of the Marine Corps
To: Distribution List

Subj: Standing Operating Procedures for Marine Corps Air
      Station Search and Rescue (SAR) Units and Helicopter SAR
      Crewmember Evaluation and Training Program

Ref: (a) NWP 19
      (b) OPNAVINST 3710.7L
      (c) NWP19-1
      (d) NATO Search and Rescue Manual (ATP-10)
      (e) OPNAVINST 3130.6
      (f) MCO P3500.17, Aviation Training and Readiness
          Manual (T&R Manual, Volume 4)
      (g) NAVMEDCOMINST 1510.5 (NOTAL)
      (h) OPNAVINST 5442.2E
      (i) MCO 4630.16B
      (j) NWP 19-2 (NOTAL)
      (k) MAC Helicopter Operations (MACR 55-54) (NOTAL)
      (l) Cold Weather Operations (OH5-3.1) (NOTAL)

Encl: (1) Unit Category Assignments
      (2) Unit SAR Evaluation and Assist Visit Outline
      (3) Helicopter Pilot Search and Rescue (SAR) Training
          Requirements
      (4) Helicopter Pilot SAR Evaluation
      (5) Helicopter Rescue Swimmer Training and Proficiency
          Requirements
      (6) Helicopter Rescue Swimmer Evaluation
      (7) Pilots Evaluation and Assist Visit Checklist
      (8) Rescue Swimmer and Paraloft Evaluation and Assist
          Visit Checklist
      (9) Listing of Possible SAR Equipment for Prepositioning
          in Duty SAR Aircraft
      (10) Airfield Operations Duty Officer SAR Briefing Form
      (11) Injury Alphabetic Codes
      (12) Use of Assets for Civilian SAR Assistance
      (13) Rescue Report

1. _Purpose._ To establish basic guidance for the prosecution
of any noncombat SAR mission by United States Marine Corps
units responsible for SAR and to establish and promote
standardization for Marine Corps helicopter units SAR capable
responsibilities. Additionally this Order provides the
relationship and coordination between USMC SAR units and other
SAR agencies per reference (a).

2. _Background._ Per references (a) through (d) and as
required by reference (e), USMC SAR units and Marine Corps
helicopter squadrons have a wide responsibility for providing
rescue capability. This dispersion of responsibility and a
review of past SAR efforts, existing procedures, and
qualification requirements indicate the need for a noncombat
helicopter rescue procedure standardization program within the
United States Marine Corps.

3. _Scope._ This Order applies to all Marine Corps units
supporting rescue capable helicopters under the operational and
administrative cognizance of the Commander, Naval Air Force,
Atlantic; Commander, Naval Air Force, Pacific; and the
Commandant of the Marine Corps.

4. _Discussion._ References (a) and (d) established the
requirement for SAR units. The SAR units listed in enclosure
(1) as category A units, maintain a year round 24-hour day
helicopter SAR capability for their respective operating areas.
These operating areas can be obtained by consulting local
airfield standing operating procedures (SOP) for air
operations. SAR units provide supplemental SAR capability for
their respective coordinated Coast Guard district and support
inland SAR by providing support for the United States Air Force
per reference (a). SAR units normally maintain the capability

of providing utility helicopter support on a required basis throughout their respective airfield operating area. During normal airfield operating hours, the SAR units located at Marine Corps air stations will maintain a SAR response status in consonance with each local air station's requirements. After normal operating hours, on weekends and holidays, or at the conclusion of tactical flying, the local air stations will relax the SAR response status as required.

5. General

    a. References (a) through (f) establish basic SAR procedures, pilot and rescue swimmer training, proficiency requirements, and requirements for designation as a Helicopter Rescue Swimmer or Rescue Aircrewman.

    b. This Order publishes policy regarding the following:

        (1) SAR pilot and rescue swimmer or rescue aircrewman requirements and employment.

        (2) An evaluation and assist visit program to promote standardized SAR procedures within individual units and throughout the helicopter community per reference (e).

        (3) Procedures for organization and maintenance of a Marine Corps air station SAR unit.

    c. Annual SAR Unit Evaluation and Assist Visit criteria are outlined in enclosure (2) and amplified in enclosures (3) through (8). The SAR pilot and rescue swimmer training requirements, delineated by enclosures (3) and (5), amplify those requirements published in references (b) and (f).

    d. Station Operations and Engineering Squadron, Marine Corps Air Station (MCAS), Cherry Point SAR is designated the USMC SAR Evaluation Unit. It is the responsibility of this unit to administer an annual SAR evaluation for all USMC units which are established primarily to fulfill SAR mission responsibilities. Additionally, the SAR responsibilities in conjunction with other mission areas.

6. Definitions

    a. Rescue Capable Helicopters. All helicopter aircraft equipped and configured with rescue hoist and rescue gear. Only those helicopters additionally configured with a doppler system are considered capable of night over water rescue.

    b. SAR Evaluation. An evaluation of the training and readiness of units assigned a primary mission of SAR (i.e., MCAS SAR units). This evaluation is conducted on an annual basis by the Marine Corps SAR Evaluation Unit per enclosure (2).

    c. SAR Assist. An assist visit shall consist of a review of the training and readiness of FMF units which may be assigned SAR responsibilities in conjunction with other mission areas. This assist visit is conducted prior to a long term unit deployment and will be conducted by the USMC SAR Evaluation Unit or a USMC SAR unit per enclosure (2).

    d. Category A Unit. An activity whose primary assigned mission is SAR. Unit category assignments are listed in enclosure (1).

    e. Category B Unit. An activity which may be assigned to provide SAR services. Unit category assignments are listed in enclosure (1).

7. SAR Training/Standardization Program

    a. SAR Qualified Crew (Category A). Crews assigned to SAR missions shall be fully qualified for SAR per this Order and the appropriate Naval Air Training and Operating Procedures Standardization (NATOPS) flight manual. The helicopter aircraft commander (HAC) shall have completed a helicopter pilot initial SAR training syllabus containing requirements in references (b), (f), and enclosure (3) of this Order, and other requirements that may be delineated by local instructions. The copilot shall have completed an approved SAR School; i.e.,

U.S. Navy SAR School, HC-16, Naval Air Station (NAS), Pensacola, Florida, and the SAR ground training syllabus specified in enclosure (3). The crew chief shall be NATOPS qualified and have completed the training requirements per reference (f). For HH-46 night missions over water, the HAC and copilot shall be current per NATOPS requirements for night approaches to a doppler assisted hover.

    b. <u>SAR Qualified Crew (Category B)</u>. Crews assigned to SAR missions shall be fully qualified for SAR per this Order and the applicable NATOPS flight manual. The HAC shall have a thorough understanding of SAR procedures and SAR requirements in reference (b), and comply with local command requirements.

    c. <u>Rescue Swimmer</u>

    (1) Helicopters assigned a primary mission of SAR over water, air station coastal SAR, shall be adequately manned, equipped, and prepared to place a rescue swimmer in the water to assist the survivor. The rescue swimmer shall have completed a helicopter rescue swimmer initial SAR training syllabus and be currently qualified per references (b), (f), and enclosure (5) of this Order. An embarked rescue swimmer shall be appropriately attired per references (b) and (c) and prepared for deployment to avoid delay when:

        (a) Engaging in an active SAR mission, or
        (b) Participating as plane guard during actual launch and recovery cycles.

    (2) It is desirable that all rescue capable aircraft operating over water be capable of conducting SAR operations. On those flights when a qualified rescue swimmer is embarked, he should have all equipment required for water entry aboard the aircraft. This policy is not intended to preclude the assignment of airborne helicopters not manned with a rescue swimmer to the prosecution of a SAR mission when other assets are not available or when multiple search platforms are required.

    (3) <u>Rescue Swimmer Deployment.</u> The rescue swimmer shall enter the water and assist the survivor(s) in all cases except when the aircraft commander determines that the circumstances will unnecessarily endanger the rescue swimmer. Factors to be considered include sea state, debris in water, sea predators, or surface burning oil or fuel. The rescue swimmer shall be deployed by either jumping or use of the rescue hoist. During night operations, or when other hazards exist in the vicinity, the rescue swimmer shall be lowered via hoist.

    (4) <u>Open Ocean Rescue Swimmer Deployment</u>

        (a) Night instrument meteorological conditions (IMC) open ocean rescue swimmer deployment is permitted only during actual SAR evolutions. Rescue swimmers shall not be deployed for night or IMC open ocean recovery of inanimate objects.

        (b) Standards of operations safety for day or visual meteorological conditions (VMC) open ocean rescue swimmer deployment for training shall include as a minimum:

        <u>1</u> A lifeboat in visual contact with the rescue swimmer(s) undergoing training. The boat shall carry an armed marksman, a rescue swimmer, and be in constant two-way radio communications with the rescue helicopter. A lifeboat is most desirable while training helicopterborne rescue swimmers; however, a second helicopter airborne and in visual contact with the rescue swimmer(s) is an acceptable substitute if operational commitments dictate.

        <u>2</u> Sea state of 2 or less.
        <u>3</u> Ceiling/visibility of at least 1000'/three nautical miles.
        <u>4</u> Antiexposure suits shall be worn per references (b) and (c).

    d. <u>SAR In-Flight Medical Technician (IFMT)</u>. SAR units shall be adequately manned, equipped, and trained to perform rappel and hoist operations to place an IFMT to assist survivors. The IFMT shall have completed Naval Aircrew Candidate school,

Rappelling school, and be a qualified Navy enlisted code 8294 per references (b), (f), and (g). IFMT's assigned to units with a primary mission of over water SAR are exempt from the Rappel school and training requirements.

e. Commanding Officers of Marine Corps Helicopter Squadrons or Units

(1) Shall designate, in writing, a naval aviator as the Command SAR Officer (for category A units).

(2) Shall designate, in writing, a Command SAR Standardization Instructor (where rescue swimmers are assigned).

(3) Shall establish and complete SAR pilot and rescue personnel training and requirements per references (b) and (f), and enclosures (3) and (5) (for category A units).

(4) Shall schedule an annual evaluation with the USMC SAR Evaluation Unit (for category A units).

(5) Shall schedule an assist visit with the nearest available USMC SAR unit prior to long term amphibious deployments (for category B units).

f. Command SAR Officer (Category A Units)

(1) Shall attend an approved SAR School; i.e., U.S. Navy SAR School, HC-16, NAS Pensacola, Florida.

(2) Shall be responsible for maintaining an operational SAR capability through the training, qualification, and proficiency requirements under the criteria set forth in reference (b) and enclosures (3) and (5).

(a) Shall fly an annual SAR evaluation flight with the USMC SAR Evaluation Unit and ensure that each pilot has an annual SAR evaluation (may be conducted concurrently with NATOPS check).

(b) Shall conduct pilot SAR ground training biannually. A written ground training syllabus and lecture series covering the areas specified by reference (b) and enclosure (4) is required by reference (e).

(c) The Command SAR Officer shall ensure that all SAR training is conducted per reference (f) and a SAR training flight is flown at least quarterly by each pilot. (The prosecution of an actual SAR may be documented as SAR training.)

(3) Shall ensure rescue swimmers complete initial qualifications within 90 days of reporting to the command after completing Rescue Swimmer School.

(4) Shall ensure that all SAR directives and manuals are current and available to all pilots and rescue swimmers.

(5) Shall ensure documentation and maintenance of all SAR training and proficiency records for each pilot and rescue swimmer.

g. Command SAR Standardization Instructor (Category A Units)

(1) Shall be designated, in writing, by the commanding officer.

(2) Shall be annually evaluated by the USMC SAR Evaluation Unit. A copy of the evaluation shall be filed in the individual's NATOPS Flight Personnel Training and Qualification Jacket in part B of section 2, Qualifications and Achievements.

(3) Shall be responsible for the training and indoctrination of all rescue swimmers per references (b) and (f), and enclosure (5).

(4) Shall conduct an annual evaluation on each rescue swimmer assigned to the command. Guidelines for conducting the rescue swimmer evaluation are contained in enclosure (6).

(5) Shall ensure documentation of all SAR training and that proficiency records are maintained on each rescue swimmer.

h. SAR Evaluation Unit

(1) Shall conduct SAR unit evaluations.

(2) Shall function as the coordinator and point of contact for matters pertaining to noncombat SAR.

i. MCAS SAR Units. Shall conduct SAR assist visits for deploying helicopter units prior to deployment.

8. SAR Operations

a. Emergency Communications Systems. The SAR helicopter will be manned as directed by local SOP by all duty crewmembers when notification of an in-flight emergency is received over the air station crash circuit. The duty SAR pilots will tune their radios to the assigned frequency for further instructions and/or monitor the progress of the in-flight emergency. The duty SAR aircraft commander may choose to launch at his discretion during the progress of the in-flight emergency. He is not obligated to launch until notified that an actual aircraft mishap has occurred or when directed by a member of the operational chain of command.

b. SAR Recall

(1) The SAR aircraft commander will provide the operations duty officer with a recall list of the duty SAR crew to include a telephone page number (i.e., Beeper), if used.

(2) Crewmembers will notify the operations duty officer when they are away from their residential telephone and using the pager recall system.

(3) In all conditions, local airfield procedures will take precedence and prevail.

c. Crew Duty Times. Crew duty times shall follow requirements in reference (b) and local airfield procedures.

d. Normal SAR Procedures

(1) The primary rescue vehicle shall be either a SAR configured HH-46A or UH-1N helicopter. All aircraft assigned for SAR shall have operable equipment required in reference (h) and enclosure (9). For over water SAR, the HH-46A should be equipped with an operable doppler with hover coupler and, if installed, an operable Loran C Navigation Receiver; the UH-1N should be equipped with operable stabilization and automatic hover equipment. Utilization of the HH-46 hover coupler shall be at the discretion of the SAR HAC. Day/night hover operations are prohibited in all situations where the pilot has insufficient visual cues, either natural or artificial, to maintain a stabilized hover, unless the appropriate hover equipment is utilized.

(2) The crew for (category A) over water SAR missions shall consist of two SAR qualified pilots, a SAR crewchief, a SAR IFMT, and a SAR rescue swimmer. A SAR rescue swimmer is not required for overland rescue operations. During normal airfield operating hours, the duty SAR crew will be located per local SOP and prepared for a rapid launch. When a SAR alert commences, the SAR crew will receive a phone brief from the airfield operations duty officer or, if airborne, from an air traffic control facility. The briefing form provided in enclosure (10) will be used.

(3) In all emergency launch situations, the ultimate authority to launch the duty SAR aircraft lies with the commanding officer or his representative and the SAR HAC.

(4) Per reference (a), upon arrival over the mishap site or survivor, the SAR aircraft should declare himself "On Scene Commander," arrange an altitude for the radio relay aircraft, and send home any aircraft which can no longer be of assistance.

(5) For survivors in the water, the SAR rescue swimmer will be deployed. Rescue swimmer deployment will be per reference (c).

(6) The SAR IFMT or SAR rescue swimmer will be deployed for land survivors. The IFMT is preferred for overland deployment.

(7) Civilians involved with a SAR mission, who are not authorized to fly in Government aircraft by reference (i), may ride in the SAR helicopter when authorized by the commanding officer. These passengers must sign a release of responsibility form (DD-1381), prior to flight. This form shall not be taken on the flight and shall remain with a responsible authority.

(8) When a rescue has been accomplished, the respective airfield operations department shall be notified by radio concerning survivor disembarkation location, the expected time of arrival, and survivor condition. Enclosure (11) may be used to avoid passing information on casualty injury classification in plain language. Airfield operations departments will provide this information to appropriate medical personnel.

e. General Procedures

(1) As prescribed by reference (a), the Search and Rescue Mission Coordinator (SMC) shall be designated in writing. The Rescue Coordination Center will be manned and equipped as required. For all SAR incidents within maritime regions, USMC SAR units will respond in coordination with their respective Coast Guard district. Additionally, USMC SAR units will respond for all inland SAR incidents in coordination with Headquarters, Aerospace Rescue and Recovery Service, Air Force Coordination center, Scott Air Force Base, Illinois. The HAC of the primary alert crew is to assume "On Scene Commander" of each SAR mission involving military aircraft. Exceptions to the SAR on scene commanders include Coast Guard coordinated and controlled SAR missions or the presence of a more suitable SAR vehicle on the scene.

(2) Closed field operations are authorized for SAR aircraft at their home stations under visual meteorological conditions only. Reference (b) provides amplifying guidance.

(3) A complete SAR crew shall be airborne in the duty SAR helicopter for all flights conducted by that aircraft.

(4) Enclosure (12) provides information for use of military assets for civilian SAR assistance.

f. SAR Personnel Responsibilities (Category A Units)

(1) Officer in Charge of SAR

(a) Ensure the readiness of SAR personnel and equipment (other than the basic aircraft inventory).

(b) Submit duty rosters of SAR personnel as required by local policy.

(c) Ensure that pilot and aircrew in-flight and ground training are conducted per references (a), (b), (c), (e), and (f), as applicable.

(d) Ensure that the Rescue Report required by reference (c) is submitted following all rescues, rescue attempts, and assists. The Rescue Report should be submitted to: SAR Model Manager, HC-16, NAS, Pensacola, Florida 32508-5600. The Rescue Report form is provided as enclosure (13), and should be used unless directed otherwise by higher authority.

(e) Ensure pilots assigned for SAR duty as HAC attend the Navy SAR School, HC-16, Pensacola, Florida.

(f) Coordinate with the aircraft maintenance officer to ensure:

<u>1</u> A helicopter qualified for the mission per reference (h) is assigned as the duty SAR helicopter.

<u>2</u> A helicopter qualified for the mission per reference (h) is assigned as the backup helicopter.

<u>3</u> The duty and standby helicopter are equipped with the proper rescue equipment required for the mission. Reference (c) provides a list of SAR equipment for tailoring the SAR aircraft to preposition overland or offshore, as the mission dictates.

(g) Ensure that a written SAR ground training syllabus exists per reference (e).

(h) Ensure that aircrew training is conducted and appropriately logged in Aircrew Performance Record.

(i) Assign a noncommissioned officer in charge (NCOIC) for SAR.

(2) <u>SAR Pilots</u>

(a) SAR pilots are responsible to the airfield operations officer and the officer in charge (OIC) of SAR for the performance of their SAR duties.

(b) All SAR pilots will undertake the initiative to remain current per references (a) through (f), as applicable.

(3) <u>NCOIC of SAR</u>

(a) The NCOIC of SAR is responsible to the OIC of SAR for enlisted aircrew training. This responsibility will include (but is not limited to):

<u>1</u> The design and execution of all enlisted aircrew training (coordinated with senior aircrewmembers).

<u>2</u> Maintaining Aircrew Performance Records for each enlisted aircrewmember.

(b) The NCOIC of SAR is responsible for review and preparation of all SAR rescue equipment.

(c) The NCOIC of SAR will prepare and update current recall rosters for all SAR personnel. These rosters will be distributed as required by local policy.

(d) The NCOIC of SAR is responsible to the OIC of SAR for maintenance and update of the SAR training and readiness data system as maintained by local policy.

(4) <u>Senior Crewchief.</u> The senior crewchief is responsible to the OIC of SAR for the training and proficiency of all SAR crewchiefs. This training will be accomplished per reference (f).

(5) <u>Senior Rescue Swimmers.</u> The senior rescue swimmer is responsible for the training and proficiency of all rescue aircrewmen. This will be accomplished per paragraph 7b.

(6) <u>Senior IFMT.</u> The senior IFMT is responsible to the OIC of SAR for the training and proficiency of all SAR IFMT's. This will be accomplished per references (f) and (g).

(7) <u>SAR Crewmen</u>

(a) The SAR crewmen are responsible to the OIC of SAR for their individual duties.

(b) The duty SAR crewchief is directly responsible to the OIC and NCOIC of the SAR unit for the daily operational aspects of the duty aircraft.

(c) The senior enlisted aircrewmember shall be responsible to the SAR HAC for the conduct of the enlisted SAR duty crew.

g. <u>SAR Units Requiring Rappel Qualified Personnel</u>

(1) Those SAR units operating in mountainous areas should maintain SAR rescue aircrewmen rappel certified. Normally these rescue aircrewmen will be Navy corpsmen also used as IFMT's.

(2) For standardization purposes throughout the Navy and Marine Corps, those SAR units maintaining rappel qualified personnel should attend Helicopter Aircrew Rappelling Indoctrination course, number D050-2006, NAS Pensacola, Florida. This school is administered by HC-16, the Navy SAR Model Manager.

h. <u>Water Bucket Operations</u>

(1) Each USMC SAR unit having aircraft capable of lifting heloborne water buckets shall provide support for local and station fire fighting requirements per local agreements and directives.

(2) To support this fire fighting effort, local support agreements shall be drawn between civilian fire agencies and forestry services for fire bucket support operations.

i. <u>References for Further SAR Assistance.</u> References (j) through (l) provide additional SAR procedures and details and should be maintained and reviewed by all USMC air station SAR units.

9. <u>Guide to List Enclosures.</u> Enclosures (1) through (13) exist to assist the SAR aircrew in different aspects of SAR throughout the Marine Corps. This listing is not all inclusive, and aircrews should consult the actual listed references for amplifying directions.

10. <u>Recommendation for Improvement.</u> This Order is intended to provide stability of training procedures and standardization of operating procedures while remaining responsive to new techniques and ideas. Recommendations for improvement of SAR related matters should be directed to the CMC (ASA) via the USMC SAR Evaluation Unit and an assist visit unit.

11. <u>Reserve Applicability.</u> This Order is applicable to the Marine Corps Reserve.

K. A. SMITH
Deputy Chief of Staff
for Aviation

DISTRIBUTION: L12 plus 7000016 (30)

Copy to: 8145001

UNIT CATEGORY ASSIGNMENTS

CATEGORY A

MCAS Cherry Point SAR
MCAS Beaufort SAR
MCAS Kaneohe Bay SAR
MCAS Iwakuni SAR
MCAS El Toro SAR
MCAS Yuma SAR

CATEGORY B

HMM 165	HMM 268
HMM 262	HMT 301
HMM 265	HMH 361
HMM 364	HMH 363
HMH 463	HMH 462
HML 167	HMH 465
HMT 204	HMH 466
HMM 261	HMA 169
HMM 264	HML 267
HMM 266	HMT 303
HMH 362	HML 367
HMH 461	HMA 369
HMM 162	HMM 764
HMM 263	HML 767
HML 269	HML 771
HMM 365	HMH 772
HMH 464	HMH 772 DET A & B
HMM 161	HMM 774
HMM 163	HML 776
HMM 164	HMX 1
HMM 166	

UNIT SAR EVALUATION AND ASSIST VISIT OUTLINE

1. Unit SAR evaluations and assists visits conducted by USMC SAR units shall consist of the following:

    a. Review of SAR publications.

    b. Review of command SAR plan and SAR SOP.

    c. Review of SAR ground and flight training syllabi.

    d. Review of pilot training records.

    e. Written examination for all SAR HAC's as outlined in enclosure (3). (Category A units.)

    f. Evaluation of SAR officer and one other pilot selected at random consisting of a SAR brief and flight as outlined in enclosure (3). (Category A units.)

    g. Review of enlisted aircrew SAR ground and flight training syllabi.

    h. Review of enlisted aircrew NATOPS training records.

    i. Review of personnel service records for appropriate entries.

    *j. Evaluation of SAR Standardization Instructor and assistant, if applicable, consisting of pool and flight phase as outlined in enclosure (5).

    *k. Evaluation of all available command rescue swimmers' personal equipment and rescue procedures during the pool phase.

    *l. Written examination for all command rescue swimmers as outlined in enclosure (5).

    *m. Inspection of aircraft SAR equipment and SAR equipment maintenance procedures.

    n. Review of the command's manning documents.

    * Applicable only to commands assigned rescue swimmers.

2. Each of the above areas will be assigned a point value. At the completion of the evaluation, the total point value and numerical grade of the command will be objectively computed as outlined in enclosures (7) and (8).

3. A debrief shall be held following the evaluation and assist visit with the unit commanding officer and other personnel he may designate.

4. Upon completion of an annual unit SAR evaluation, the senior member of the evaluation team shall ensure the completion and forwarding of the evaluation report to the CMC (ASA) through the appropriate chain of command. A copy of the evaluation report will be forwarded to the command.

5. Upon completion of the assist visit, the senior member of the evaluation team shall ensure the completion and forwarding of the assist visit report to the unit's commanding officer. A list of repeat discrepancies will be forwarded to the unit's training officer. A list of commands completing assist visits will be forwarded to the CMC (ASA) on an annual basis.

HELICOPTER PILOT SEARCH AND RESCUE (SAR) TRAINING REQUIREMENTS

Minimum pilot SAR training requirements are specified in the current edition of OPNAVINST 3710.7 and amplified, but not limited, to the following:

1. Ground Training Lesson Guides

a. Search Planning. Including computations on parachute drift, total water current, sweep width, track spacing, probability of detection, and search patterns.

b. Capabilities and availability of Computer Assisted Search Planning (CASP), Navy Search and Rescue System (NAVSAR), and the Monterey Computer Search Planning Program.

c. Utilization and limitations of various SAR equipment.

d. Review various SAR related publications and directives; i.e., NWP-19, NWP-19-1, NWP 19-2, NWP-42, and ATP-10.

e. Review responsibilities and duties of SAR Coordinator, SAR Mission Coordinator, On-Scene Commander, and rescue units.

f. Local area familiarization including landmarks, medical facilities with helicopter pads or other designated landing areas, and course rules.

g. Review geographic and weather factors and their effects on search planning.

h. Review local SAR organization:

(1) Command SAR Plan to include as a minimum: Command SAR responsibility to the local area, SAR procedures, frequency plan, and coordination and relationship to local agencies able to render assistance; i.e., U.S. Coast Guard, U.S. Air Force, and other military and civilian authorities.

(2) SAR procedures to include as a minimum: alerting procedures, recall procedures, launch procedures, and procedures pertaining to rescue reports.

2. Flight Training

a. Aircrew Brief. Including situations, weather, search areas, patterns, altitude, communications, and lookout scanner techniques.

b. Search Patterns. Including day, night, over water, and overland; i.e., expanding square sector search, parallel search, tactical air navigation (TACAN) arcing, tactical navigation (TACNAV) search plans, etc. Ship, air, and shore coordination as applicable.

c. On-Scene Commander Duties. Including traffic control, search organization, communication and problem solving; i.e., track spacing, probability of detection, endurance, etc.

d. Helicopter Approaches. Including day and night doppler and nondoppler approaches per applicable aircraft NATOPS flight manual.

e. Conduct actual or simulated helicopter rescue swimmer deployment and pickup.

f. Local area familiarization emphasizing hospital landing pads, SAR units, etc.

g. Completion of requirements as set forth in the current edition of MCO P3500.17 for category A units only.

h. Completion of required syllabus flights as required by appropriate and applicable training and readiness manuals for category B units.

<u>HELICOPTER PILOT SAR EVALUATION</u>
A written examination shall be given by the USMC SAR
Evaluation Team to all command helicopter pilots (category A).
An oral and flight evaluation shall be given to the command SAR
officer and one pilot selected at random (category A units
only). The topics listed below outline those subjects which
will be covered during this evaluation.

1. <u>Written and Oral Evaluation Topics</u>

    a. Search Planning

       (1) Drift (sea and wind current, leeway)

       (2) Sweep width

       (3) Track spacing

       (4) Probability of detection

       (5) SAR publications

    b. Search Patterns

       (1) Trackline search

       (2) Creeping line search

       (3) Parallel search

       (4) Sector search

       (5) Expanding square search

       (6) Parallel arcing (TACAN)

       (7) TACNAV (if installed)

    c. Knowledge of Area

       (1) Area topography and landmarks

       (2) Area facilities

    d. Local SAR organization

    e. SAR equipment

    f. Land and rough terrain searches

    g. Climatic effects on SAR

       (1) IMC and low visibility

       (2) Heat or Cold

    h. Responsibilities of SAR Coordinator, SAR Mission
Coordinator, On-Scene Commander, and SAR unit.

2. The flight evaluation shall be conducted using a simulated
accident scenario with the pilot under evaluation acting as
on-scene commander.

    a. SAR Brief

       (1) Crew coordination and responsibilities

        (2) Scanning procedures

        (3) Emergency procedures

        (4) Crew SAR and survival

    b. Mission Execution

        (1) Search planning

            (a) Area knowledge

            (b) Sweep width and track spacing

            (c) Search pattern selection

        (2) Search pattern execution

        (3) Crew coordination

        (4) On-Scene commander coordination

        (5) Voice procedures

HELICOPTER RESCUE SWIMMER TRAINING AND PROFICIENCY REQUIREMENTS

1. Helicopter Rescue Swimmer Initial SAR Training Syllabus:
The rescue swimmer initial training syllabus is primarily
designed to acclimate the rescue swimmer to the new aircraft
and locale. This is considered a minimum syllabus and commands
are encouraged to supplement this syllabus with additional
lectures and materials pertinent to local mission requirements.
To be initially qualified as a rescue swimmer in a new command
the individual must meet requirements of the current editions
of OPNAVINST 3710.7, NWP 19-1, and:

    a. Perform a minimum of 6-day water entry jumps from a
helicopter to a simulated survivor, three of which must be from
the same model aircraft as the swimmer's parent command.

    b. Perform a minimum of two night water entries from an
aircraft to a simulated survivor in a controlled environment.
One entry must be from the same model aircraft as operated by
the swimmer's parent command. (Commands capable of night
over water rescue.)

    c. Complete all requirements as delineated in the current
edition of MCO P3500.17.

    d. Complete a standardization check by the Command SAR
Standardization Instructor.

    e. Be designated in writing by the unit commanding officer
as a helicopter rescue swimmer for that command.

    f. Personnel reporting to commands as rescue swimmers
shall complete the requirements of the current edition of MCO
P3500.17 training syllabus within 90 days after completing
Rescue Aircrewman School.

2. Helicopter Rescue Swimmer Annual SAR Proficiency and
Evaluation Requirements. Minimum annual SAR proficiency
requirements for helicopter rescue swimmers are specified in
the current edition of OPNAVINST 3710.7; the following list
amplifies those requirements.

    a. Requalification in Coronary Pulmonary Resuscitation
(CPR) based upon annual written test and demonstration of
proficiency verified by a qualified CPR instructor.

    b. Six-day water entry jumps which shall be from the
command's aircraft to an actual or simulated survivor.

    c. Two night water entries which shall be from the
command's aircraft to an actual or simulated survivor.
(Commands capable of night over water rescue.)

    d. Four hours of in-water training every 6 months to
practice lifesaving techniques which shall include:

        (1) Rescue swimmer equipment utilization

        (2) Approaches

        (3) Releases

        (4) Carries

        (5) Parachute disentanglement - day

        (6) Parachute disentanglement - night

NOTE: The commanding officer may grant written waivers of the
       above 6-month requirements under special circumstances
       which may preclude their completion.

    e. Complete a rescue swimmer evaluation by the Command SAR
Standardization Instructor as outlined in the current edition
of OPNAVINST 3710.7 and enclosure (5).

f. Completion of the above requirements shall be accomplished within 12 calendar months of the previous evaluation. Failure to complete proficiency requirements and obtain a rating of qualified, will require a reevaluation within 30 days. Rescue swimmers who fail to meet currency requirements within 30 days and fail the reevaluation shall appear before a squadron/unit evaluation board. That board after consideration of all circumstances shall recommend one of the following courses of action.

(1) A period of training (not to exceed 6 months) to be followed by a reevaluation. This option may be utilized when extenuating circumstances such as medical grounding, TAD to schools, etc., have precluded maintenance of currency or physical conditioning. During the training period the rescue swimmer shall not be considered qualified for actual rescue situations.

(2) Removal from a flying status.

ENCLOSURE (5)

HELICOPTER RESCUE SWIMMER EVALUATION

Using the format listed below, unit SAR standardization instructors shall conduct an annual rescue swimmer evaluation on each rescue swimmer within the command. This same format shall be utilized by the USMC SAR Evaluation Team, during SAR evaluations.

1. A written examination covering:

    a. First aid

    b. Personal SAR equipment

    c. Platform rescue equipment

    d. Rescue procedures and survivor's equipment

    e. Rescue swimmer hand signals

2. Oral evaluation (normally administered concurrently with the practical evaluation.)

3. Practical evaluation including:

    a. Flight phase:

        (1) Rescue swimmer deployment

        (2) Rescue hand signals

        (3) Water emergencies

        (4) Rescue swimmer recovery

    b. Pool phase:

        (1) Lifesaving procedures

        (2) Parachute disentanglement

        (3) Rescue devices

ENCLOSURE (6)

PILOTS EVALUATION AND ASSIST VISIT CHECKLIST

COMMAND: DATE:

_____   _____

EVAL TEAM SENIOR MEMBER: DATE OF EVAL/ASSIST VISIT:

_____   _____

COMMAND SAR OFFICER: DATE OF LAST EVAL/ASSIST VISIT:

_____   _____
                                         _____

GRADE KEY:

QUALIFIED (Q)	= 4.0	
CONDITIONALLY QUALIFIED (CQ)	= 2.0	
UNQUALIFIED (U)	= 0.0	

1. SAR OFFICER: Q   CQ   U   POINTS

    A. DESIGNATION LETTER   _____
    B. SAR SCHOOL GRADUATE   _____
        (CAT A ONLY)
                              _____
                              SUB AREA POINTS   = TOTAL
        NUMERICAL AREA GRADE NUMBER OF SUB AREAS   POINTS

2. SAR PUBLICATIONS: Q   CQ   U   POINTS

    A. NWP 19   _____
    B. NWP 19-1 AND NWP 19-2 _____
    C. NWP 42 (SERIES)   _____
    D. NWP 55-8-SAR   _____
        (SAR TACAID) (SERIES)
    E. OPNAVINST 3130.6   _____
    F. OPNAVINST 3710.7   _____
        (SERIES)
        NUMERICAL AREA GRADE TOTAL POINTS

3. COMMAND SAR PLAN: Q   CQ   U   POINTS

                              _____

    A.   RESPONSIBILITY TO THE
        LOCAL AREA

    B.   FREQUENCY PLAN   _____
    C.   OTHER AGENCIES ABLE TO
        ASSIST   _____
        NUMERICAL AREA GRADE   TOTAL POINTS

4. COMMAND SAR SOP:	Q	CQ	U	POINTS
A. ALERTING PROCEDURES				
B. RECALL PROCEDURES				
C. LAUNCH PROCEDURES				
D. RESCUE REPORTING				
NUMERICAL AREA GUIDE		TOTAL POINTS		

5. GROUND TRAINING SYLLABUS:	Q	CQ	U	POINTS
A. SEARCH PLANNING				
B. SAR EQUIPMENT				
C. SAR PUBLICATIONS				
D. SC, SMC, OSCSRU (RESPONSIBILITIES)				
E. LOCAL AREA FAMILIARIZATION				
F. GEOGRAPHICAL AND WEATHER FACTORS				
G. COMMAND SAR PLAN AND SOP				
NUMERICAL AREA GRADE	SUB AREA POINTS = TOTAL	NUMBER OF SUB AREAS POINTS		

6. DOCUMENTATION OF GROUND TRAINING:	Q	CQ	U	POINTS
FREQUENCY OF GROUND TRAINING				
NUMERICAL AREA GRADE		TOTAL POINTS		

7. FLIGHT TRAINING SYLLABUS:	Q	CQ	U	POINTS

ENCLOSURE (7)

A.   AIRCREW BRIEF

B.   SC, SM, OSC, SRU
     RESPONSIBILITIES   _____
C.   SEARCH PATTERNS   _____
D.   APPROACHES   _____
E.   SWIMMER DEPLOYMENT/
     RECOVERY
                                            _____
     NUMERICAL AREA GRADE   TOTAL POINTS

8. DOCUMENTATION OF FLIGHT TRAINING: PILOT AND COPILOT	Q	CQ	U	POINTS

NUMERICAL AREA GRADE   TOTAL POINTS

9. INDIVIDUAL SAR EVALUATION: ANNUAL (CAT A ONLY)	Q	CQ	U	POINTS

NUMERICAL AREA GRADE   TOTAL POINTS

10. WRITTEN EXAMINATION: (CAT A ONLY)	Q	CQ	U	POINTS
OVERALL GRADE POINT AVERAGE				

     NUMERICAL AREA GRADE   TOTAL POINTS

11. ORAL EVALUATION (CAT A ONLY)	Q	CQ	U	POINTS
A. SCANNING TECHNIQUES				
B. SEARCH PATTERNS C. SC, SM, OSC, SRU				
D. SEARCH PLANNING				

     NUMERICAL AREA GRADE   TOTAL POINTS

12. FLIGHT EVALUATION (CAT A ONLY) A. SEARCH PATTERNS	Q	CQ	U	POINTS
B. SWIMMER DEPLOYMENT				

C. SURVIVOR PICKUP

D. CREW COORDINATION

      NUMERICAL AREA GRADE   TOTAL POINTS

SECTIONS	Q	CQ	U	SECTION GRADE x WT FACT	SUMMARY FINAL GRADE
1. SAR OFFICER				X1	
2. SAR PUBLICATIONS				X1	
3. COMMAND SAR PLAN				X2	
4. COMMAND SAR SOP				X2	
5. GROUND TRAINING SYLLABUS				X2	
6. DOCUMENTATION OF GROUND TRAINING				X2	
7. FLIGHT TRAINING				X2	
8. DOCUMENTATION OF FLIGHT TRAINING				X2	
9. INDIVIDUAL SAR EVALUATION (CAT A)				X1	
10. WRITTEN EVALUATION (CAT A ONLY)				X2	
11. ORAL EVALUATION (CAT A ONLY)				X1	
12. FLIGHT EVALUATION (CAT A ONLY)				X2	
				X 15/20	

OVERALL GRADE KEY

QUALIFIED	=	4.00
CONDITIONALLY QUALIFIED	=	2.00
UNQUALIFIED	=	0.00

OVERALL GRADE = FINAL SECTIONS GRADE TOTAL

COMMAND GRADE =   WT. FACTOR TOTAL

ENCLOSURE (7)

RESCUE SWIMMER AND PARALOFT EVALUATION AND ASSIST VISIT
CHECKLIST

COMMAND: DATE:

_____   _____

EVAL TEAM SENIOR MEMBER: DATE OF EVAL/ASSIST VISIT:

_____   _____

COMMAND SAR STANDARDIZATION   DATE OF LAST EVAL/ASSIST VISIT:
INSTRUCTOR:

_____   _____

COMMAND SAR STANDARDIZATION
 INSTRUCTOR:

_____

COMMAND ASST. SAR   AVIATION/EQUIPMENT SHOP
STANDARDIZATION INSTRUCTOR: SUPERVISOR:

_____   _____

GRADE KEY:
                    QUALIFIED (Q)   = 4.0
                    CONDITIONALLY QUALIFIED (CQ)   = 2.0
                    UNQUALIFIED (U)   = 0.0

_____

                                  Q   CQ   U   POINTS
1.   MANNING DOCUMENTS
     NUMERICAL AREA GRADE   _____

                                  TOTAL POINTS

_____

2.   ENLISTED PERSONNEL SERVICE   Q   CQ   U   POINTS
     RECORDS

NUMERICAL AREA GRADE   TOTAL POINTS

_____

  3. NATOPS TRAINING JACKETS   Q   CQ   U   POINTS

     A.   FLIGHT PHYSICAL   _____

     B.   SIX DAY JUMPS   _____

     C.   TWO NIGHT DEPLOYMENTS   _____

     D.   ANNUAL CPR CERTIFICATION
                                  _____

                E.   ANNUAL 8 HOURS POOL
          TRAINING
                                  _____

     F.   ANNUAL SAR EVALUATION
          REPORTS
                                  _____

     G.   RESCUE SWIMMER
          DESIGNATION LETTERS
                                  _____

                                      ENCLOSURE (8)

                    1

H. GROUND TRAINING

NUMERICAL AREA GRADE	SUB AREA NUMBER OF SUB AREAS	= TOTAL POINTS

4. PARLOFT - SAR EQUIPMENT	Q	CQ	U	POINTS
A. HISTORY CARDS				
B. DOUBLE RESCUE HOOK				
C. RESCUE STRAP (HORSE COLLAR)				
D. QUICK SPLICE				
E. CABLE GRIP				
F. PNEUMATIC RESCUE HAND TOOL				
G. CHEM LIGHTS AND ATTACHING STRAPS				
H. HEAVY DUTY GLOVES				
I. TWO WOOL BLANKETS				
J. RESCUE EQUIPMENT CASE				
K. TRAIL LINE ASSEMBLY				
L. RESCUE LITTER SLING				
M. MEDICAL KIT				
N. FOREST PENETRATOR				
O. RESCUE SEAT				
P. RESCUE NET				
Q. SAR I VEST				
R. ANTIEXPOSURE SUIT				
S. RESCUE HARNESS				
T. CURRENT RESCUE EQUIPMENT AIRCRAFT EQUIPMENT CUSTODY CARDS				

NUMERICAL AREA GRADE	SUB AREA POINTS POINTS OF SUB AREAS	= TOTAL POINTS

5. INDIVIDUAL SAR EVALUATION (CAT A ONLY)	Q	CQ	U	POINTS
A. SAR SWIMMER EQUIPMENT				
B. WRITTEN EXAMINATION				

ENCLOSURE (8)

C.   ORAL EVALUATION

D.   POOL PHASE   _____

E.   FLIGHT PHASE   _____

     NUMERICAL AREA GRADE   _____

                                   TOTAL POINTS

                          SECTION GRADE SUMMARY

SECTIONS	Q	CQ	U	x WT FACT	FINAL GRADE
1. MANNING DOCUMENTS				X 1	
2. ENLISTED PERSONNEL SERVICE RECORDS				X 1	
3. NATOPS TRAINING JACKETS				X 2	
4. PARALOFT				X 2	
5. INDIVIDUAL SAR EVALUATION (CAT A ONLY)				X 1	
				X 7	

OVERALL GRADE KEY

QUALIFIED	=	4.00
CONDITIONALLY QUALIFIED	=	2.00
UNQUALIFIED	=	0.00

OVERALL GRADE = <u>FINAL SECTIONS GRADE TOTAL</u>
                    WT. FACTOR TOTAL

COMMAND GRADE =

ENCLOSURE (8)

3

INDIVIDUAL SAR SWIMMERS EQUIPMENT STATUS

Date: _____

Command: _____

The column headings read vertically down the form:

```
Command:   | | | | | | | | | | | |M|S| | | |
           | | | | | | | | | | | |K|T| | | |
           | | | | | |A| | | | | |-|R| |C| |
           | | | | | |T| | |S|"|1|O|B|H| |
        |W| | | | | |T|H|L|K|J|3|O|L|E| |P
        |E| |B| | | |A|B|P|B|"| |E|U|M|S|A
        |T| |O| | | |C|U|U| | |F| |E|L|N|R
        | | |O|M| | |H|-|-|K|K|L|L|I|O|A
        |S|H|T|I|F|M|M|1|2|N|N|A|I|L|R|
        |U|O|I|T|I|A|E|1|8|I|I|R|G|E|K|B
        |I|O|E|T|N|S|N|/|/|F|F|E|H|N|E|A
NAME|RATE|T|D|S|S|S|K|T|P|P|E|E|S|T|S|S|L|G
```

Decoded column headings (left to right):

NAME	RATE	WETSUIT	HOOD	BOOTIES	MITTS	FINS	MASK	ATTACHMENT	HBU-11/P	LPU-28/P	SKBKNIFE	"J"KNIFE	MK-13 FLARES	STROBE LIGHT	CHEMLIGHTS	BLUE LIGHTS	SNORKEL	PARABAG
____	____																	
____	____																	
____	____																	
____	____																	
____	____																	
____	____																	
____	____																	
____	____																	
____	____																	
____	____																	
____	____																	
____	____																	
____	____																	
____	____																	
____	____																	
____	____																	
____	____																	
____	____																	
____	____																	
____	____																	
Total Equipment Discrepancies:																		

Key: A - Adjustment
      C - Corroded
      M - Missing
      N - Not Complete
      R - Needs Repair
      S - Satisfactory
      U - Equipment Unavailable for Inspection

ENCLOSURE (8)

Date: _____

_____ COMPLETED THE FOLLOWING RESCUE SWIMMER
TRAINING ON THE ABOVE DATE.

A. APPROACH PROCEDURES

    _____ FRONT SURFACE

    _____ REAR SURFACE

    _____ UNDERWATER

B. CARRY PROCEDURES

    _____ CROSS CHEST

    _____ COLLAR TOW/EQUIPMENT

    _____ TIRED SWIMMER

C. RELEASE PROCEDURES

    _____ FRONT HEAD HOLD

    _____ ALTERNATE FRONT HEAD HOLD

    _____ REAR HEAD HOLD

    _____ ALTERNATE REAR HEAD HOLD

D. OTHER PROCEDURES

    _____ TOWER JUMPS/AIRCRAFT JUMPS

    _____ DAY PARACHUTE DISENTANGLEMENT

    _____ NIGHT PARACHUTE DISENTANGLEMENT

    _____ STOKES LITTER WORK

    _____ MAN OVERBOARD CONSCIOUS/UNCONSCIOUS

E. FIRST AID PROCEDURES

    _____ CPR/MOUTH TO MOUTH BREATHING

    _____ BLEEDING

    _____ SPLINTING/BANDAGING

    _____ HEAD/NECK/BACK INJURIES

    _____ HEAT INJURIES/COLD INJURIES

COMMENTS: _____

_____

_____

_____

USMC SOES
HELICOPTER RESCUE SWIMMER
SEARCH AND RESCUE
EVALUATION REPORT

NAME	GRADE	SSN	DATE		
TOTAL WATER ENTRIES	TYPE AIRCRAFT		DATE OF LAST EVALUATION		
REQUIREMENT	DATE COMPLETED		GRADE		
			Q	CQ	U
WRITTEN EXAMINATION					
LIFESAVING PROCEDURES					
PARACHUTE DISENTANGLEMENT					
RESCUE DEVICES					
SWIMMER DEPLOYMENT					
RESCUE HAND SIGNALS					
EMERGENCY					
SWIMMER RECOVERY					

GRADE, NAME OF USMC SAR EVALUATOR/INSTRUCTOR	SIGNATURE	DATE
GRADE, NAME OF EVALUEE	SIGNATURE	DATE

REMARKS OF UNIT SAR OFFICER

GRADE, NAME OF UNIT SAR OFFICER	SIGNATURE	DATE

ENCLOSURE (8)

LISTING OF POSSIBLE SAR EQUIPMENT FOR PREPOSITIONING
IN DUTY SAR AIRCRAFT

Basic Equipment

Double rescue hook
Rescue strap (Horse Collar)
One quick splice
One cable grip (chicago grip) with crewman safety belt
One rescue hand tool (pneumatic webbing/cable cutter)
Crewman safety belts
Four high-intensity chemical lights with two rescue hook
chemical light straps
One pair of heavy duty gloves
Cranials as needed
Two wool blankets
One helicopter rescue equipment case
One trail assembly
One rescue litter sling assembly
One Level B medical kit (Corpsman) or A for (Rescue Swimmer)

Additional Over water SAR Equipment

2 MK-58 smoke flares
6 MK-25 smoke flares
3 Electrical sea marker lights
1 Electrical datum marker
3 LPP-1 life preservers
Rescue litter sling assembly
Aldis lamp
Hoisting vest
Rescue litter assembly
Coast Guard rescue basket
Rescue net

Equipment Required for Rapelling

1 E3 - 250 descent control system
2 14G - 0 Large sky genie descent devices (w/PG carabiners)
2 E3 - type sky genie descent harness
2 L3 - 150 1/2" descent rope 2/locking carabiners
1 L3 - 100 1/2" descent rope 2/locking carabiners
4 ISC - 2 canvas bags

Additional SAR Equipment for Overland

4 MK-18 smoke flares
3 Crewman safety belts
Aldis lamps
One shovel
4 Nylon straps (3 straps 6' long, 1 strap 12' long)
Two flashlights
1 Level B medical kit (Corpsman use)
Climber's Spikes
Climber's rope (one 150')
10 Carbiners
1 Figure eight descender
Forest penetrator
4 Stubai Model 85 steel "O" locking carabiners
1 Sky genie escape/rescue system
1 spring loaded stitch belay plate
4 Stubai chrome cadmium steel carabiners
1 Pair mountain boots

Mountainous Terrain Equipment

Cold weather apparel
2 man tent
2 bugaboo sleeping bags
10 snow flukes
1 candle
C-rations

ENCLOSURE (9)

AIRFIELD OPERATIONS DUTY OFFICER SAR BRIEFING FORM

The following form shall be used by SAR participants as a convenient single source of SAR gathering information.

1. Time: _____

2. Distressed craft/vessel: _____

3. Position of emergency (latitude/longitude) mishap location:
_____

4. Nature of emergency: _____
_____

5. Survivors sighted? _____

6. Parachute sighted? _____

7. Craft description (size, type, hull color, cabin color, rigging, fuselage color, tail color, wingtip color): _____
_____
_____

8. Persons on board/clothing description: _____
_____

9. Date, time, and point of departure, planned route - Emergency vessel: _____
_____
_____

10. Radio frequencies in use, monitored: _____

11. Emergency radio equipment and frequencies: _____

12. On scene WX (cloud coverage, rain, severe WX, visibility, sea state): _____
_____
_____

13. Assistance desired: _____

14. Assistance received: _____

15. Search area designation: _____
_____

16. Commence search point: _____

17. Search area boundaries: _____

18. Search pattern: _____Creep: _____

19. Air/Air TACAN: _____

20. En route search is/is not desired? _____

INJURY ALPHABETIC CODES

Injury classifications are defined below. Alfa, Bravo, Charlie, Delta, Lima, and Uniform are defined injuries for mishap severity level classification.

a. <u>Alfa</u> - Fatal Injury. An injury which results in death from a mishap or the complications arising therefrom, regardless of the length of time intervening between the mishap and a subsequent death.

b. <u>Bravo</u> - Permanent Total Disability. Any nonfatal injury which, in the opinion of competent medical authority, permanently and totally incapacitates a person to the extent that they cannot follow any gainful occupation. In addition, the loss of, or the loss of use of, both hands, both feet, both eyes, or a combination of any of these body parts as a result of a single mishap will be considered as a permanent total disability.

c. <u>Charlie</u> - Permanent Partial Disability. An injury which does not result in death or permanent total disability but, in the opinion of competent medical authority, results in permanent impairment or loss of any part of the body, the loss of the great toe, the thumb, or unrepairable inguinal hernia, with the following exceptions:

   (1) Teeth

   (2) The four smaller toes

   (3) Distal phalanx of any finger

   (4) Repairable hernia

   (5) Hair, skin, nails, or any subcutaneous tissue

d. <u>Delta</u> - An injury which does not result in death, permanent total disability, or permanent partial disability, but which results in one or more lost workdays (not including the day of injury).

e. <u>Echo</u> - Bodily harm requiring greater than first aid (but not involving a lost workday).

f. <u>Foxtrot</u> - Bodily harm requiring only first aid, or no treatment.

g. <u>Golf</u> - No bodily harm.

h. <u>Lima</u> - Lost at sea.

i. <u>Uniform</u> - Missing or unknown.

USE OF ASSETS FOR CIVILIAN SAR ASSISTANCE

1. Launch for civilian assistance by USMC SAR units, will be on a not-to-interfere basis with the airfield SAR commitment. Normal alert notice will be through the airfield operations officer of his representative.

2. All civilians needing medical assistance will be transported as directed by the SAR mission coordinator. If aircrews are uncertain, civilians will be transported to the respective military hospital for processing and further transportation. All civilians not requiring medical attention will be returned to respective airfield with the SAR aircraft or as directed by the SAR mission coordinator.

3. Remains of deceased individuals will not be removed from the mishap site unless preservation of the corpse is in question. Otherwise, all remains should be turned over to the sheriff's department, county coroner, or U.S. Coast Guard representative on scene.

ENCLOSURE (12)

COMPLETION INSTRUCTIONS

1. Indicate aircraft reporting custodian, ship or facility controlling search and rescue unit (SRU).

2. Supply the specific type of vehicle, such as SH-3H, DDG, motor whaleboat, etc.

2.a. Actual total number of flight hours expended on the SAR case by the SRU.

2.b. Actual total number of steaming hours expended on the SAR case by the SRU.

2.c. Actual total number of aircraft sorties expended on the SAR case by the SRU.

2.d. Actual total number of ship sorties expended on the SAR case by the SRU.

3. Number by calendar year; i.e. 84-01 would be the first report for 1984.

4. Indicate the military command, Government agency or civilian activity requesting assistance.

5. Provide the U.S. Air Force Rescue Coordination Center mission number or Coast Guard unit case number, if assigned.

6.a. The complete date time group of each mission phase is to be provided in the appropriate blank. (Use local time.)

6.b. Self-explanatory.

7. Check all appropriate blocks that apply to this mission.

8. Self-explanatory.

9.a. Grade/Rate, if military.

9.b. Billet, pilot, copilot, swimmer, hospital corpsman, etc.

10. Check appropriate box and circle item or items as applicable. Be sure to identify equipment "needed" in recommendations section (block 17).

10.a. Check as appropriate and circle equipment items as applicable. Justify equipment "needed" in recommendations section (block 17).

10.b. Check as appropriate and circle equipment items as applicable. Justify equipment "needed" in recommendations section (block 17).

10.c. Self-explanatory, but be sure to explain in detail under problems encountered section (block 16).

11. Fill in appropriate number in each block.

12. Fill in each block with number of personnel in each category.

13. This should include a brief narrative of distress situation which initiated the mission, including aircraft and/or vessel types, location, weather, and how rescue units were alerted.

14. This should include SRU SAR posture/alert status and search tactics. Explain how the search was planned and if applicable, search patterns, track spacing, sweep widths, probability of detection for each search, and assumptions made in planning (i.e., LR1 life raft with a drogue for an over water ejection).

15. Explain how the recovery was effected. This section may also be used to provide amplifying comments regarding rescue equipment used and medical treatment provided.

16. Explain any difficulties encountered (i.e., personnel, weather, mechanical, communications, etc.).

17. These should be brief and explicit.

18. Self-explanatory.

19.a. Self-explanatory.

19.b. Indicate number of applicable deployments in number block.

19.c. Explain in detail any appropriate Rescue Swimmer Problems/Recommendations.

www.ingramcontent.com/pod-product-compliance
Lightning Source LLC
Chambersburg PA
CBHW080627290526
45790CB00007B/2960